The Funny Side

Sometimes humor is the best way to communicate.

SCHOLASTIC

LITERACY PLACE®

Copyright acknowledgments and credits appear on page 128, which constitutes an extension of this copyright page.

Copyright © 1996 by Scholastic Inc.   All rights reserved.   Printed in the U.S.A.
ISBN 0-590-49110-5

5 6 7 8 9 10   24   02 01 00 99 98 97

Step into
a Cartoonist's Studio

Sometimes humor is the best way to communicate.

A Laugh a Day

Our sense of humor lets us find funny stories in everyday events.

"All your wishes shall be granted," cried the fairy.
"Ziz Ziz Boom, Tic Tac Ta,
This empty can shall be a car."

What's So Funny?

Surprise and exaggeration can make things seem funny.

Oodles of Noodles

Funny People

People use humor to entertain each other.

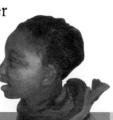

Trade Books

The following books accompany *The Funny Side* SourceBook.

AWARD WINNING Book

Chocolate-Covered Ants

by Stephen Manes

AWARD WINNING Book

The Cybil War

by Betsy Byars

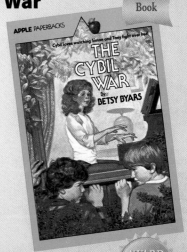

AWARD WINNING Book

James and the Giant Peach

by Roald Dahl illustrated by Nancy Ekholm Burkert

AWARD WINNING Book

The Stinky Cheese Man

by Jon Scieszka illustrated by Lane Smith

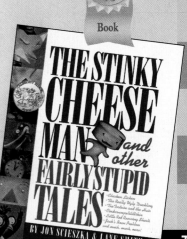

Our sense of humor lets us find funny stories in everyday events.

A Laugh a Day

Meet Fudge, who gets the family into one sticky situation after another. Then find out why laughing is good for you.

Visit a cartoonist's studio and learn what makes people laugh.

Discover what space aliens think about a popular pet.

W ORKSHOP 1

Choose a favorite fairy tale and create your own fractured fairy tale.

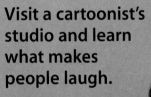

"All your wishes shall be granted," cried the fairy. "Ziz Ziz Boom, Tic Tac Ta, This empty can shall be a car."

from

TALES OF A FOURTH GRADE NOTHING

Mr. and Mrs. JUICY-O

by

JUDY BLUME

illustrated by

LIZ CALLEN

One night my father came home from the office all excited. He told us Mr. and Mrs. Yarby were coming to New York. He's the president of the Juicy-O company. He lives in Chicago. I wondered if he'd bring my father another crate of Juicy-O. If he did I'd probably be drinking it for the rest of my life. Just thinking about it was enough to make my stomach hurt.

My father said he invited Mr. and Mrs. Yarby to stay with us. My mother wanted to know why they couldn't stay at a hotel like most people who come to New York. My father said they could. But he didn't want them to. He thought they'd be more comfortable staying with us. My mother said that was about the silliest thing she'd ever heard.

But she fixed up Fudge's bedroom for our guests. She put fancy sheets and a brand-new blanket on the hide-a-bed. That's a sofa that opens up into a bed at night. It's in Fudge's room because that used to be our den. Before he was born we watched TV in there. And lots of times Grandma slept over on the hide-a-bed. Now we watch TV right in the living room. And Grandma doesn't sleep over very often.

My mother moved Fudge's crib into my room. He's going to get a regular bed when he's three, my mother says. There are a lot of reasons I don't like to sleep in the same room as Fudge. I found that out two months ago when my bedroom was being painted. I had to sleep in Fudge's room for three nights because the paint smell made me cough. For one thing, he talks in his sleep. And if a person didn't know better, a person could get scared. Another thing is that slurping noise he makes. It's true that I like to hear it when I'm awake, but when I'm trying to fall asleep I like things very quiet.

When I complained about having to sleep with Fudge my mother said, "It's just for two nights, Peter."

"I'll sleep in the living room," I suggested. "On the sofa . . . or even a chair."

"No," my mother said. "You will sleep in your bedroom. In your own bed!"

There was no point in arguing. Mom wasn't going to change her mind.

She spent the day in the kitchen. She really cooked up a storm. She used so many pots and pans Fudge didn't have any left to bang together. And that's one of his favorite pastimes—banging pots and pans together. A person can get an awful headache listening to that racket.

Right after lunch my mother opened up the dinner table. We don't have a separate dining room. When we have company for dinner we eat in one end of the living room. When Mom finished setting the table she put a silver bowl filled with flowers right in the middle. I said, "Hey, Mom . . . it looks like you're expecting the President or something."

"Very funny, Peter!" my mother answered.

Sometimes my mother laughs like crazy at my jokes. Other times she pretends not to get them. And then, there are times when I know she gets them but she doesn't seem to like them. This was one of those times. So I decided no more jokes until after dinner.

I went to Jimmy Fargo's for the afternoon. I came home at four o'clock. I found my mother standing over the dinner table mumbling. Fudge was on the floor playing with my father's socks. I'm not sure why he likes socks so much, but if you give him a few pairs he'll play quietly for an hour.

I said, "Hi, Mom. I'm home."

"I'm missing two flowers," my mother said.

I don't know how she noticed that two flowers were missing from her silver bowl. Because there were at least a dozen of them left. But sure enough, when I checked, I saw two stems with nothing on them.

"Don't look at me, Mom," I said. "What would I do with two measly flowers?"

So we both looked at Fudge. "Did you take Mommy's pretty flowers?" my mother asked him.

"No take," Fudge said. He was chewing on something.

"What's in your mouth?" my mother asked.

Fudge didn't answer.

"Show Mommy!"

"No show," Fudge said.

"Oh yes!" My mother picked him up and forced his mouth open. She fished out a rose petal.

"What did you do with Mommy's flowers?" She raised her voice. She was really getting upset.

Fudge laughed.

"Tell Mommy!"

"Yum!" Fudge said. "Yummy yummy yummy!"

"Oh no!" my mother cried, rushing to the telephone.

She called Dr. Cone. She told him that Fudge ate two flowers. Dr. Cone must have asked what kind, because my mother said, "Roses, I think. But I can't be sure. One might have been a daisy."

There was a long pause while my mother listened to whatever Dr. Cone had to say. Then Mom said, "Thank you, Dr. Cone." She hung up.

"No more flowers!" she told Fudge. "You understand?"

"No more," Fudge repeated. "No more . . . no more . . . no more."

My mother gave him a spoonful of peppermint-flavored medicine. The kind I take when I have stomach pains. Then she carried Fudge off to have his bath.

Leave it to my brother to eat flowers! I wondered how they tasted. *Maybe they're delicious and I don't know it because I've never tasted one,* I thought. I decided to find out. I picked off one petal from a pink rose. I put it in my mouth and tried to chew it up. But I couldn't do it. It tasted awful. I spit it out in the garbage. Well, at least now I knew I wasn't missing anything great!

Fudge ate his supper in the kitchen before our company arrived. While he was eating I heard my mother remind him, "Fudgie's going to be a good boy tonight. Very good for Daddy's friends."

"Good," Fudge said. "Good boy."

"That's right!" my mother told him.

I changed and scrubbed up while Fudge finished his supper. I was going to eat with the company. Being nine has its advantages!

My mother was all dressed up by the time my father got home with the Yarbys. You'd never have guessed that Mom spent most of the day in the kitchen. You'd also never have guessed that Fudge ate two flowers. He was feeling fine. He even smelled nice—like baby powder.

Mrs. Yarby picked him up right away. I knew she would. She looked like a grandmother. That type always makes a big deal out of Fudge. She walked into the living room cuddling him. Then she sat down on the sofa and bounced Fudge around on her lap.

"Isn't he the cutest little boy!" Mrs. Yarby said. "I just love babies." She gave him a big kiss on the top of his head. I kept waiting for somebody to tell her Fudge was no baby. But no one did.

My father carried the Yarbys' suitcase into Fudge's room. When he came back he introduced me to our company.

"This is our older son, Peter," he said to the Yarbys.

"I'm nine and in fourth grade," I told them.

"How do, Peter," Mr. Yarby said.

Mrs. Yarby just gave me a nod. She was still busy with Fudge. "I have a surprise for this dear little boy!" she said. "It's in my suitcase. Should I go get it?"

"Yes," Fudge shouted. "Go get . . . go get!"

Mrs. Yarby laughed, as if that was the best joke she ever heard. "I'll be right back," she told Fudge. She put him down and ran off to find her suitcase.

She came back carrying a present tied up with a red ribbon.

"Ohhhh!" Fudge cried, opening his eyes wide. "Goody!"
He clapped his hands.

Mrs. Yarby helped him unwrap his surprise. It was a
windup train that made a lot of noise. Every time it bumped
into something it turned around and went the other way.
Fudge liked it a lot. He likes anything that's noisy.

I said, "That's a nice train."

Mrs. Yarby turned to me. "Oh, I have something for you too uh . . . uh. . . ."

"Peter," I reminded her. "My name is Peter."

"Yes. Well, I'll go get it."

Mrs. Yarby left the room again. This time she came back with a flat package. It was wrapped up too—red ribbon and all. She handed it to me. Fudge stopped playing with his train long enough to come over and see what I got. I took off the paper very carefully in case my mother wanted to save it. And also to show Mrs. Yarby that I'm a lot more careful about things than my brother. I'm not sure she noticed. My present turned out to be a big picture dictionary. The kind I liked when I was about four years old. My old one is in Fudge's bookcase now.

"I don't know much about big boys," Mrs. Yarby said. "So the lady in the store said a nice book would be a good idea."

A nice book would have been a good idea, I thought. *But a picture dictionary! That's for babies!* I've had my own regular dictionary since I was eight. But I knew I had to be polite so I said, "Thank you very much. It's just what I've always wanted."

"I'm so glad!" Mrs. Yarby said. She let out a long sigh and sat back on the sofa.

My father offered the Yarbys a drink.

"Good idea . . . good idea," Mr. Yarby said.

"What'll it be?" my father asked.

"What'll it be?" Mr. Yarby repeated, laughing. "What do you think, Hatcher? It'll be Juicy-O! That's all we ever drink. Good for your health!" Mr. Yarby pounded his chest.

"Of course!" my father said, like he knew it all along. "Juicy-O for everyone!" my father told my mother. She went into the kitchen to get it.

While my father and Mr. Yarby were discussing Juicy-O, Fudge disappeared. Just as my mother served everyone a glass of Mr. Yarby's favorite drink he came back. He was carrying a book—my old, worn-out picture dictionary. The same as the one the Yarbys just gave me.

"See," Fudge said, climbing up on Mrs. Yarby's lap. "See book."

I wanted to vanish. I think my mother and father did too.

"See book!" Now Fudge held it up over his head.

"I can use another one," I explained. "I really can. That old one is falling apart." I tried to laugh.

"It's returnable," Mrs. Yarby said. "It's silly to keep it if you already have one." She sounded insulted. Like it was my fault she brought me something I already had.

"MINE!" Fudge said. He closed the book and held it tight against his chest. "MINE . . . MINE . . . MINE. . . ."

"It's the thought that counts," my mother said. "It was so nice of you to think of our boys." Then she turned to Fudge. "Put the book away now, Fudgie."

"Isn't it Fudgie's bedtime?" my father hinted.

"Oh yes. I think it is," my mother said, scooping him up. "Say goodnight, Fudgie."

"Goodnight Fudgie!" my brother said, waving at us.

Fudge was supposed to fall asleep before we sat down to dinner. But just in case, my mother put a million little toys in his crib to keep him busy. I don't know who my mother thought she was fooling. Because we all know that Fudge can climb out of his crib any old time he wants to.

He stayed away until we were in the middle of our roast beef. Then he came in carrying Dribble's bowl. He walked right up to Mrs. Yarby. He thought she was his new friend. "See," he said, holding Dribble under her nose. "See Dribble."

Mrs. Yarby shrieked. "Ohhhh! I can't stand reptiles. Get that thing away from me!"

Fudge looked disappointed. So he showed Dribble to Mr. Yarby. "See," he said.

"HATCHER!" Mr. Yarby boomed. "Make him get that thing out of here!"

I wondered why Mr. Yarby called my father "Hatcher." Didn't he know his first name was Warren? And I didn't like the way Mr. and Mrs. Yarby both called Dribble a "thing."

I jumped up. "Give him to me!" I told Fudge. I took Dribble and his bowl and marched into my room. I inspected my turtle all over. He seemed all right. I didn't want to make a big scene in front of our company but I was mad! I mean *really* mad! That kid knows he's not allowed to touch my turtle!

"Peter," my father called, "come and finish your dinner."

When I got back to the table I heard Mrs. Yarby say, "It must be interesting to have children. We never had any ourselves."

"But if we did," Mr. Yarby told my father, "we'd teach them some manners! I'm a firm believer in old-fashioned good manners!"

"So are we, Howard," my mother said in a weak voice.

I thought Mr. Yarby had a lot of nerve to hint that we had no manners. Didn't I pretend to like their dumb old picture dictionary? If that isn't good manners, then I don't know what is!

My mother excused herself and carried Fudge back to my room. I guess she put him into his crib again. I hoped she told him to keep his hands off my things.

We didn't hear from him again until dessert. Just as my mother was pouring the coffee he ran in wearing my rubber gorilla mask from last Hallowe'en. It's a very real-looking mask. I guess that's why Mrs. Yarby screamed so loud. If she hadn't made so much noise my mother probably wouldn't have spilled the coffee all over the floor.

My father grabbed Fudge and pulled the gorilla mask off him. "That's not funny, Fudge!" he said.

"Funny," Fudge laughed. "Funny, funny, funny Fudgie!"

"Yes sir, Hatcher!" Mr. Yarby said. "Old-fashioned manners!"

By that time I'm sure my father was sorry the Yarbys weren't staying at a hotel.

I finally got to bed at ten. Fudge was in his crib slurping away. I thought I'd never fall asleep! But I guess I did. I woke up once, when Fudge started babbling. He said, "Boo-ba-mum-mum-ha-ba-shi." Whatever that means. I didn't even get scared. I whispered, "Shut up!" And he did.

Early the next morning I felt something funny on my arm. At first I didn't wake up. I just felt this little tickle. I thought it was part of my dream. But then I had the feeling somebody was staring at me. So I opened my eyes.

Fudge was standing over me and Dribble was crawling around on my arm. I guess Fudge could tell I was about ready to kill him because he bent down and kissed me. That's what he does when my mother's angry at him. He thinks nobody can resist him when he makes himself so lovable. And a lot of times it works with my mother. But not with me! I jumped up, put Dribble back into his bowl, and smacked Fudge on his backside. *Hard*. He hollered.

My father came running into my room. He was still in his pajamas.

He whispered, "What's going on in here?"

I pointed at Fudge and he pointed at me.

My father picked up my brother and carried him off. "Go back to sleep, Peter," he said. "It's only six o'clock in the morning."

I fell asleep for another hour, then woke up to an awful noise. It was Fudge playing with his new train. It woke up everybody, including the Yarbys. But this time there was nobody they could blame. They were the ones who gave Fudge the train in the first place.

Breakfast was a quiet affair. Nobody had much to say. Mr. Yarby drank two glasses of Juicy-O. Then he told my father that he and Mrs. Yarby had their suitcases packed. They were leaving for a hotel as soon as breakfast was over.

My father said he understood. That the apartment was too small for so many people. My mother didn't say anything.

When Mr. Yarby went into Fudge's bedroom to pick up his suitcase his voice boomed. "HATCHER!"

My father ran toward the bedroom. My mother and Mrs. Yarby followed him. I followed them. When we got there we saw Fudge sitting on the Yarbys' suitcase. He had decorated it with about one hundred green stamps. The kind my mother gets at the supermarket.

"See," Fudge said. "See . . . pretty." He laughed. Nobody else did. Then he licked the last green stamp and stuck it right in the middle of the suitcase. "All gone!" Fudge sang, holding up his hands.

It took my mother half an hour to peel off her trading stamps and clean up the Yarbys' suitcase.

The next week my father came home from the office and collected all the cans of Juicy-O in our house. He dumped them into the garbage. My mother felt bad that my father had lost such an important account. But my father told her not to worry. Juicy-O wasn't selling very well at the stores. Nobody seemed to like the combination of oranges, grapefruits, pineapples, pears, and bananas.

"You know, Dad," I said. "I only drank Juicy-O to be polite. I really hated it!"

"You know something funny, Peter?" my father said. "I thought it was pretty bad myself!"

SOURCE

SCHOLASTIC NEWS

News Magazine

Laughing is Good for You!

by Karen Burns
illustrated by Tim Haggerty

AWARD WINNING Magazine

Imagine that you've had a really stressful day. You didn't do so hot on your history test. You forgot your gym clothes. And, to make matters worse, Dad packed liverwurst in your lunch!

How do you beat the stress and brighten up your day? Maybe a really great joke or a funny movie will do the trick. Doctors have been studying what happens inside our bodies when we laugh. They believe that getting the giggles can help us beat stress and stay healthy. Here's why:

When you first start to laugh, your heart beats very quickly. But after a few seconds, your heartbeat slows down a lot. That makes you feel very relaxed. Some doctors also think that when you laugh, your brain makes chemicals

WHAT DOES AN APATOSAURUS DO WHEN IT SLEEPS?

DINO-SNORES!

ZZZZZZZZZZZ...

called endorphins (en-DOOR-fins). These chemicals may help kill pain and make you feel happy. A good belly laugh is also good exercise for your heart. Experts say that laughing about 100 times a day gives your heart the same workout as rowing a boat for ten minutes!

For hospitals and nursing homes, this is news to smile about. Many of these places are starting to use clowns and carts full of comedy tapes, funny games, and joke books to help their patients get better. Kids know the power of humor, too. Fourth graders in Oceanside, New York, recently wrote a book full of comics, limericks, and jokes for patients in a local nursing home.

So remember, a few laughs a day can keep the doctor away.

Robb Armstrong

Cartoonist

Making people *laugh* is all in a *day's work.*

Robb Armstrong is a cartoonist whose comic strip "Jump Start" appears in 150 newspapers across the country. During the day, Armstrong is an art director at an advertising agency. Mornings, evenings, and weekends he draws his comic strip. He has deadlines each week, when all his strips for the following week have to be handed in. The Joe and Marcy characters in "Jump Start" may lead busy lives, but Armstrong is kept even busier creating them.

PROFILE

Name: Robb Armstrong

Occupation: cartoonist and art director

Favorite cartoon characters in fourth grade: Fred Flintstone and Snoopy

Childhood idol: Charles Schulz, creator of "Peanuts"

Cartoon created in fourth grade: "Praying Mantis Man," an African-American superhero

Funniest joke: "Never mind. It's so dumb, my wife leaves the room every time I tell it."

29

QUESTIONS
for Robb Armstrong

Find out how *Robb Armstrong* turned a talent for drawing into a *career.*

Q **How did you become interested in being a cartoonist?**

A I began drawing when I was four years old. Like many kids, I loved to draw, and I decided to stick with it. When I was 17, I sold some political cartoons to the *Philadelphia Tribune.* I thought I had found an easy career. It wasn't until later that I realized how much work it would take to be a professional cartoonist.

Q **Did you continue to draw cartoons in college?**

A When I went to Syracuse University, I worked on the school paper, *The Daily Orange.* I did a strip called "Hector." Having to draw a comic strip every day meant that I had to be organized and self-disciplined. The experience taught me a lot and helped me later in life.

Q **Is it difficult to get a new comic strip published?**

A It took me a good ten years to achieve any kind of success. The field of syndicated comics—comics which appear in newspapers all over the country—is very competitive. I finally got a yearlong development deal with United Features Syndicate. This meant I had a year in which to come up with a successful strip.

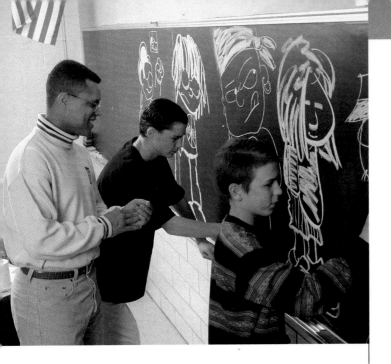

Q **Why do you like to visit schools and talk about your career?**

A I enjoy visiting schools almost as much as drawing. I want kids to know that they can have dreams. I tell them that everyone has a talent— that's the easy part. Building a talent, that's what takes hard work.

Q **How did you think up the characters Joe and Marcy?**

A My editor suggested I think about characters that I know best. Eventually, I drew the characters Joe and Marcy, a young black couple with busy careers. Joe might be a cop and Marcy a nurse, but they're a lot like me and my wife, Sherry.

Robb Armstrong's
Tips for Cartoon Ideas

Q **Where do your ideas for jokes in the strip come from?**

A Sometimes an idea comes from radio or TV. But I think the best ideas come from life.

1 Watch how people act in different situations.

2 Listen to the way people talk, the stories they tell one another. What makes them laugh?

3 Keep a list of things that you find funny. Can you create a joke from an item on your list?

EARTH HOUNDS

AWARD
WINNING

Book

as explained by
Professor Xargle

Translated into Human by Jeanne Willis
Illustrated by Tony Ross

Good morning, class.
Today we are going to learn about Earth Hounds.

Earth Hounds have tusks in the front and a waggler at the back.

To find the tusks, dangle a sausage at each end.

Earth Hounds have buttons for eyes, a sniffer with two holes, and a built-in necktie.

They use their necktie to lick their underbellies and also the icicle cups of Earthlets who are not looking.

Earth Hounds can stand on four legs, three legs, and two legs. They can jump as high as a roast beef.

For dinner, they consume wigglemeat, skeleton biscuits, a flying snow muffin, a helping of living room rug, and a sock that is four days old.

After this feast they must be taken to a place called walkies, which has many steel trees.

The Earth Hound is attached to a string so that he can be pulled along in a sitting position.

In the park the Earthling finds a piece of tree and hurls it back and forth. The Earth Hound is made to fetch it.

Then the Earthling takes a bouncing rubber sphere and flings it into the pond.

Now the Earthling must fetch it.

The Earth Hound arrives back at the Earth Dwelling and rests under the bed covering of the Earthling.

Earth Hounds hate the hot water bowl. They tuck their wagglers between their legs and make a *Wooo-Woooooo* noise.
Once free, they dry themselves on piles of compost.

Here is a baby Earth Hound, or Houndlet, asleep in the nocturnal footwear of an Earthling.

The Earthling has placed many newspapers on the floor for the Houndlet to read.

That is the end of today's lesson.

If you are all very good, we will visit Planet Earth to play with a real Houndlet.

Those of you who would like to bring your own pets along
should sit at the back of the spaceship.

How to
Write a Fractured Fairy Tale

The fairy godmother is a young girl instead of an older woman.

Many fairy tales begin with "Once upon a time" and end with "happily ever after." What would happen if you turned a fairy tale into a fractured fairy tale?

What is a fractured fairy tale? A fractured fairy tale is a fairy tale with a twist. For example, what would happen if the Three Little Pigs became Three Big Dinosaurs, or if Sleeping Beauty decided to go back to sleep? Sometimes changing the setting is enough to add a humorous twist to the story.

Instead of a ball at the palace, there's a party at a disco.

"Bi
To t

In this story, Cinderella is a boy called Prince Cinders.

Prince Cinders wears modern clothes.

"All your wishes shall be granted," cried the fairy. "Ziz Ziz Boom, Tic Tac Ta, This empty can shall be a car."

ng Bong, Bo Bo Bo, sco you shall go!"

The fairy godmother turns an empty can into a car, instead of turning a pumpkin into a coach.

1 Choose a Fairy Tale

On your own, make a list of fairy tales that you've read or heard. If you need ideas, look through a book of fairy tales and skim the stories you know well. Read a few new ones, too. Then choose your favorite.

TOOLS

- book of fairy tales
- pencil and paper
- ruler

2 Make a Story Chart

Chart the important details of the fairy tale you chose. Who are the characters? What is the setting? What happens in the story? Study your chart, and then pick a detail or two that you would like to change. Be sure to write down any substitutions you make on your chart.

	Fairy Tale	My version
Characters	Goldilocks 3 Bears	Goldzilla The Bear Family (people)
Setting	House in woods	House in suburbs

GRIMMS' Fairy Tales

The Bears

3 Write Your Fractured Fairy Tale

If you like, begin with the traditional fairy tale opening, "Once upon a time. . . ." Use your story chart as an outline. Then rewrite the fairy tale in your own words, using your funny new twist. Are you smiling or laughing as you write? That's a sign that your audience will laugh, too. Be sure to use dialogue. It will make the story more lively.

Tips
- Change the time period of the story.
- Change the setting.
- Have a character in the fairy tale narrate the story.
- Change the characters in the story.
- Change the ending of the story.

4 Present Your Fairy Tale

When you've finished writing your fairy tale:

- Read it aloud to the class.
- Create a class book of fractured fairy tales.
- Work with a small group to turn some of the fractured fairy tales into a series of one-act plays. Invite another class to see your performance.

If You Are Using a Computer . . .

Type your fractured fairy tale on the computer, using the Sign format. Choose a border and clip art to illustrate your story.

THINK

Why does a fairy tale become humorous when you change an important part of the story?

Robb Armstrong *Cartoonist* ▶

COUNTY FAIR

PONY RIDE

STRENGTH TEST

CHAMPION HORSE

PIES

1ST

Surprise and exaggeration can make things seem funny.

What's So Funny?

Join Arthur as he tries to buy a turkey and ends up with a surprise.

Tickle your funny bone with poems and limericks.

Find out what happens when a mule decides to speak.

Meet the strongest woman in the West.

WORKSHOP 2

Make yourself laugh by writing a humorous poem.

Oodles of Noodles

I love noodles. Give me oodles.
Make a mound up to the sun.
Noodles are my favorite foodles.
I eat noodles by the ton.

Lucia and James L. Hymes, Jr.

from

The Hoboken Chicken Emergency

A Television Script
by Arthur Alsberg and Don Nelson
illustrated by Rick Brown

Based on the novel by
Daniel Manus Pinkwater

INTERIOR—BOBOWICZ LIVING ROOM—NIGHT

[POPPA snaps off the TV set as MOMMA enters, followed by ARTHUR. He reaches into his pocket and pulls out twenty dollars, which he hands to ARTHUR.]

POPPA

Arthur, that's for tomorrow morning. To pick up a turkey at O'Brien's.

MOMMA

Carl . . . How can I fit a turkey in the ice box for two weeks?

POPPA

I'm not taking any chances, and no mistakes like last year, Arthur.

ARTHUR

Why couldn't we have something else? Maybe meatloaf.

POPPA

In America, on Thanksgiving, it's turkey. Every family in the neighborhood will want a turkey—the Antonellis, the Glucksterns, the Lings, [indicating himself] . . . and the Bobowiczs. It's an American tradition.

ARTHUR

I'd rather have pizza.

POPPA

[firmly] When your grandparents were young and still in Poland, if someone said "eat turkey" they'd have to eat turkey. Here in America we have a choice. [firmly] And the choice is turkey!

EXTERIOR—PARK AND PLAYGROUND—MORNING

[ARTHUR is trudging through the park where he sees three boys playing on the swing, some distance from him.]

ARTHUR

[calling] Hey George! Hi, Benny!

[He waves, but the three boys continue swinging and don't even look over at ARTHUR. ARTHUR waits a moment . . . maybe they didn't hear him.]

ARTHUR

[calling again] Mario! Want to come to the butcher with me?

MARIO

[calling] I can't!

[The boys continue swinging, and ARTHUR turns and walks along the fence and out of the park.]

EXTERIOR—HOBOKEN STREET—MORNING

[ARTHUR stands in front of O'Brien's Meat Market. He tries the door, but it is locked. He peers through the window, but no one is inside. There is a sign in the window of the door—CLOSED BECAUSE OF A DEATH IN THE FAMILY.]

[He finally turns away, wondering what to do. Suddenly some large feathers come floating down from above. They are accompanied by a clucking sound coming from off stage. ARTHUR looks around. The clucking is not like any clucking he has ever heard before. It's deeper and louder. ARTHUR looks up toward an apartment above the meat market.]

ANOTHER ANGLE

[The second story window of the apartment. PROFESSOR MAZZOCCHI, a wild-eyed, slightly frazzled older man is leaning out the window, backwards, as if preventing something from jumping out. He notices ARTHUR in the street below.]

PROFESSOR

[calling down] Nothing to fear. Everything's under control.

[The PROFESSOR then directs his attention into the room.]

PROFESSOR

[continuing] Back! Back, Number 73!

ANGLE ON ARTHUR

[He looks up at the PROFESSOR.]

ARTHUR

Are you the butcher?

ANGLE ON PROFESSOR

PROFESSOR

[indignantly] Butcher? Me? Doctor Frankenstein was a butcher! I am a scientist!

ANGLE ON ARTHUR

ARTHUR

I came to buy our Thanksgiving turkey, but they're
closed.

ANGLE ON PROFESSOR

PROFESSOR

[his eyes widen] Money? You have some money?
Press the button next to the name "Professor
Mazzocchi."

[The PROFESSOR is distracted for a moment as he pushes something back
into the room with his foot. Then he turns back toward ARTHUR.]

PROFESSOR

[continuing; calling down] But hurry! They're going
fast!

ANGLE ON ARTHUR

[ARTHUR considers the offer, then hurries over to the entrance to the
apartment building. He looks at the card near the doorway. It reads:
PROFESSOR MAZZOCCHI—INVENTOR OF THE CHICKEN SYSTEM—BY
APPOINTMENT. ARTHUR presses the button. In a moment the buzzer sounds
to release the door. ARTHUR pushes it and enters the building.]

INTERIOR—APARTMENT LOBBY—DAY

[ARTHUR starts up the stairs but is frozen by the sound of PROFESSOR
MAZZOCCHI's voice.]

PROFESSOR (off stage)

[shouting] You will not get me evicted! My brother owns this building! I'm a scientist! If you people don't stop bothering me, I'll let the rooster loose again!

ARTHUR

[puzzled, calls] But you told me to come in.

PROFESSOR (off stage)

[realizes] Oh, it's you, my boy. Come right up. What are you waiting for?

INTERIOR HALL—TOP OF THE STAIRS—DAY

[The PROFESSOR, wearing an old bathrobe with dragons embroidered on it, greets ARTHUR as he comes up.]

PROFESSOR

The only people who ever come up here are neighbors to complain about my chickens. They don't want me to keep them.

ARTHUR

You keep chickens in your apartment?

PROFESSOR

A farm would be better, but my brother lets me stay here without paying any rent. Also, they are special chickens. I prefer to keep them under lock and key.

ARTHUR

I was supposed to get a turkey.

PROFESSOR

Do you have a large family?

ARTHUR

No, sir.

PROFESSOR

But your family has friends . . .

ARTHUR

Yes, sir. We live in a big apartment building.

PROFESSOR

Splendid! Perfect for number 73—my super chicken.

ARTHUR

My father wants a turkey.

PROFESSOR

In the spirit of Thanksgiving wouldn't your father rather feed his family and all his friends and neighbors for only . . . [stops] How much money have you got?

ARTHUR

Twenty dollars.

[ARTHUR takes the twenty dollar bill out of his pocket.]

PROFESSOR

[continuing] Just enough. Wait here.

[The PROFESSOR opens the door just enough to slide through it and closes it, leaving ARTHUR standing outside. ARTHUR stands patiently for a moment, then stirs uneasily as he hears the same loud, low clucking sound he'd heard before. Suddenly the door swings open and the PROFESSOR comes out of the apartment leading a huge chicken, taller than he is, on a leash. The CHICKEN has a look of wide-eyed innocence about her.]

PROFESSOR
The best poultry bargain on earth! One medium-sized super chicken—eight cents a pound. Here's Number 73, your two hundred and sixty-six pound super chicken.

ARTHUR
But I was supposed to get a turkey.

PROFESSOR
When I'm offering you a super chicken? Just look at this fine specimen. Good for roasting, frying, and barbecuing.

[At the sound of this the CHICKEN begins to tremble all over.]

ARTHUR
But what about my father?

PROFESSOR
Well, take it or leave it. I can always sell her to a Kiwanis picnic or the Coast Guard mess.

[ARTHUR hesitates. The CHICKEN seems to moan.]

PROFESSOR
She'll be mighty good eating.

[The CHICKEN looks over toward ARTHUR, almost pleading.]

ARTHUR

Well . . .

PROFESSOR

[quickly] A deal!

[He snaps the twenty dollars from ARTHUR's fingers and hands him the leash.]

PROFESSOR

And I'll throw in the collar and leash.

[The PROFESSOR opens the door of his apartment and disappears. ARTHUR stands there for a moment then looks up at the CHICKEN. The CHICKEN shifts from foot to foot looking rather nervous. ARTHUR, realizing his mistake, pounds on the apartment door.]

PROFESSOR (off stage)

[shouts] No refunds!

ARTHUR

Don't you have anything smaller?

PROFESSOR (off stage)

No refunds!

[ARTHUR shakes his head and looks up at the CHICKEN.]

ARTHUR

I hope Poppa likes bargains.

[He starts to lead the CHICKEN away.]

EXTERIOR—PARK AND PLAYGROUND—MORNING

[ARTHUR leads the CHICKEN along the walk as he searches the park for the three boys he had seen earlier. But the swings are empty, and no one is in sight. With a little shrug, ARTHUR accepts his lonely fate and crosses the street toward home, an old brick building with a fire escape on the outside.]

INTERIOR—APARTMENT BUILDING HALLWAY—DAY

[ARTHUR is leading the CHICKEN who follows him tamely as they climb the stairs to the second floor. ARTHUR starts down the hallway toward his apartment, then looks at the CHICKEN and stops. He has second thoughts.]

ARTHUR
[to CHICKEN] You better wait here.

[ARTHUR ties the CHICKEN to the banister and then goes to the door of his apartment. He stops and thinks for a moment. Then he enters.]

INTERIOR—BOBOWICZ LIVING ROOM—DAY

[MOMMA BOBOWICZ is vacuuming as ARTHUR enters. MOMMA looks up but continues vacuuming.]

MOMMA
What took you so long? I was starting to get worried.

ARTHUR
Are you in a good mood or a bad mood?

[ARTHUR'S MOTHER looks up at ARTHUR suspiciously then turns off the vacuum cleaner.]

MOMMA

Arthur. You didn't lose the twenty dollars?

ARTHUR

[defensively] No.

MOMMA

Good.

[ARTHUR'S MOTHER turns on the vacuum again and starts cleaning.]

ARTHUR

Not exactly.

[ARTHUR'S MOTHER turns the vacuum off again.]

MOMMA

Exactly what did you do?

ARTHUR

I got a chicken.

MOMMA

You what?

ARTHUR

You *are* in a bad mood.

MOMMA

[softening] Well, where is it?

ARTHUR

I left it in the hall. It only cost eight cents a pound.

MOMMA

That's very cheap. Are you sure there's nothing wrong with it? Maybe it isn't fresh?

ARTHUR

It's fresh all right.

[MOMMA BOBOWICZ opens the door to reveal the CHICKEN standing in the hallway tied to the banister. The CHICKEN looks toward her and clucks! MOMMA BOBOWICZ quickly closes the door and just stands there facing the closed door—speechless for a moment.]

MOMMA

There's a two hundred pound chicken in the hall!

ARTHUR

[nervously] Two hundred and sixty-six pounds.

[MOMMA BOBOWICZ is still looking at the door.]

MOMMA

Two hundred and sixty-six pounds of live chicken!
It's wearing a dog collar.

[MOMMA BOBOWICZ opens the door just a crack, peeks out, then quickly closes the door again.]

MOMMA

[continuing] It's there, all right.

[She turns toward ARTHUR accusingly.]

ARTHUR

[close to tears] I couldn't help it, Momma. I got it from this old scientist. He was saying it was a bargain, and I didn't know what to do.

[MOMMA BOBOWICZ looks at her son who is on the verge of tears. She then opens the door again and looks into the hall.]

ANGLE ON HALL

[The CHICKEN stands shifting from one foot to the other.]

ANGLE ON LIVING ROOM

[MOMMA closes the door again.]

> **ARTHUR**
>
> I thought we could call her "Henrietta."

> **MOMMA**
>
> We're not calling her anything! That twenty dollars was for a turkey to eat, not a two hundred sixty-six pound chicken to keep as a pet.

> **ARTHUR**
>
> [fighting the tears] But we can't take her back or that old man is gonna feed her to the Coast Guard or some people at a picnic. Momma, please.

[MOMMA BOBOWICZ looks at ARTHUR for a moment, thinking it over. Then she opens the door again and looks out into the hallway.]

ANGLE ON HALLWAY

[The CHICKEN looks toward MOMMA and cocks its head.]

ANGLE ON LIVING ROOM

[MOMMA looks out toward the CHICKEN and softens a bit.]

> **MOMMA**
>
> She does seem friendly, in a dumb sort of way.

[ARTHUR senses his mother's change of attitude.]

ARTHUR

I'd feed her and walk her and take care of her. I
could train her so she'd cluck if burglars ever came.

MOMMA

Well . . .

ARTHUR

Please, Momma. She's a good chicken. And I'd do
everything.

MOMMA

Who's going to tell your father?

ARTHUR

You could do that.

[ARTHUR looks at his mother innocently. She shakes her head and smiles.
It's the signal for ARTHUR to hug her gratefully.]

INTERIOR—DINING ROOM—NIGHT

[ARTHUR is seated at the dinner table with his parents. POPPA BOBOWICZ
is definitely in a bad mood.]

POPPA

You think I make money just to throw it away?

ARTHUR

I'm sorry, Poppa. I didn't mean to.

MOMMA

It's such an unusual pet, Carl. And psychologists
say it's good for the children when the family has
a pet.

POPPA

Dr. Freud should raise a family on my salary.

[ARTHUR gets up and hurries from the room.]

MOMMA

There'll still be time to get the turkey. Besides,
with what they're paying for pets these days, the
chicken's a bargain. [slyly] And everybody looks
for bargains. It's the American way.

POPPA

[seeing through it] The American way is a turkey on
the table at Thanksgiving, not a two hundred pound
chicken on a leash!

ANOTHER ANGLE TO INCLUDE ARTHUR AS HE ENTERS WITH
HENRIETTA ON THE LEASH.

ARTHUR

I'll take her back if that's what you want, Poppa.

[POPPA looks at MOMMA. She looks back, beseechingly.]

POPPA

[weakening] Well, we'll see.

[ARTHUR exchanges smiles with his mother. Then he pats HENRIETTA.
HENRIETTA looks down at a dinner plate with French fries on it. ARTHUR
holds one up for her to eat and she gobbles it down.]

POPPA

[sternly] And no feeding pets from the table.

[ARTHUR and his MOTHER react at the word "pets."]

INTERIOR—ARTHUR'S ROOM—NIGHT

[ARTHUR, in his pajamas, is standing on his bed as he talks to HENRIETTA who stands on the floor.]

ARTHUR

I've never had a chicken for a pet before. I've never even had a pet. Poppa doesn't like pets. He says they're a lot of trouble. But maybe he'll change his mind.

[HENRIETTA just looks at ARTHUR and clucks.]

ARTHUR

Come on. Jump up.

[HENRIETTA doesn't budge.]

ARTHUR

[continuing] Up on the bed, Henrietta. Up on the bed!

[HENRIETTA turns absently and starts to walk away. ARTHUR turns and closes the closet door. Startled, HENRIETTA turns and jumps on the bed. The bed collapses. ARTHUR shakes his head in dismay.]

CAMERA TERMS

DISSOLVE   the gradual replacement of one shot with another

EXTERIOR   a view of an outdoor scene

INTERIOR   a view of an indoor scene

ANGLE   the camera's point of view as it films its subject

from

Poems of A. Nonny Mouse

As I was walking round the lake,
I met a little rattlesnake.
I gave him so much ice-cream cake,
It made his little belly ache.

If you should meet a crocodile,
Don't take a stick and poke him.
Ignore the welcome in his smile,
Be careful not to stroke him.
For as he sleeps upon the Nile,
He thinner gets and thinner.
And whene'er you meet a crocodile,
He's ready for his dinner.

Selected by Jack Prelutsky
Illustrated by Henrik Drescher

A froggie sat on a lily pad,
Looking up at the sky.
The lily pad broke and the frog fell in,
Water all in his eye.

Froggy Boggy
tried to jump
on a stone
and got a bump.

It made his eyes
wink and frown
and turned his nose
upside down.

A centipede was happy quite,
Until a frog in fun
said, "Pray, which leg comes after which?"
This raised her mind to such a pitch,
She lay distracted in the ditch,
Considering how to run.

The Man in the Moon as he sails the sky
Is a very remarkable skipper,
But he made a mistake when he tried to take
A drink of milk from the Dipper.
He dipped right out of the Milky Way
And slowly and carefully filled it.
The Big Bear growled and the Little Bear howled,
And frightened him so that he spilled it!

"Bubble," said the kettle,
"Bubble," said the pot.
"Bubble, bubble, bubble,
We are getting very hot!"

Shall I take you off the fire?
"No, you need not trouble.
This is just the way we talk—
Bubble, bubble, bubble!"

from

FROM SEA TO SHINING SEA
Compiled by Amy L. Cohn

AWARD WINNING

Book

The Talking Mule

COLLECTED BY ZORA NEALE HURSTON
ILLUSTRATED BY DONALD CREWS

Old feller one time had a mule. His name was Bill. Every morning when that old feller went to catch him he'd say, "Come 'round, Bill!"

But one morning he slept late so he decided while he was drinking some coffee that he'd send his son to catch old Bill.

Told his son, "Go down there, boy, and bring that mule up here."

That boy was such a fast aleck he grabbed the bridle and went on down to the lot. When he got there, he said, "Come 'round, Bill!"

The mule looked 'round at the boy. The boy told the mule, " 'Tain't no use rollin' your eyes at me. Pa wants you this morning. Come on 'round and stick your head in this bridle."

The mule kept on looking at him and said, "Every mornin' it's 'Come 'round, Bill! Come 'round, Bill!' I can't hardly rest at night before it's 'Come 'round, Bill!'"

The boy threw down the bridle, flew back to the house, and told his pa, "That mule's talkin'!"

"Oh, come on, boy, tellin' your lies! Go on and catch that mule."

"No, sir, Pa, that mule's started to talk. You'll have to catch that mule all by yourself. I'm not goin' ta do it."

The old feller looked at his wife and said, "Do you see what a lie this boy is tellin'?"

He got up and went on down after the mule himself. When he got down to the lot he hollered, "Come 'round, Bill!"

The old mule looked 'round and said, "Every mornin' it's 'Come 'round, Bill!'"

Now, the old feller had a little dog that followed him everywhere. So when he ran for home the little dog was right behind him. The old feller told his wife, "The boy didn't tell much of a lie! That mule *is* talkin'. I've never heard a mule talk before."

L'il dog said, "Me neither."

The old feller got scared again. Right through the woods he ran with the little dog behind him. He nearly ran himself to death. Finally, he stopped, all out of breath, and said, "I'm so tired I don't know what to do."

The l'il dog caught up, sat right in front of him, panting, and said, "Me neither."

That man is running yet.

from
American Tall Tales

SALLY ANN THUNDER ANN WHIRLWIND

by Mary Pope Osborne

Wood Engravings by Michael McCurdy

NOTES ON THE STORY

THE BACKWOODS WOMEN of Tennessee and Kentucky
endured the same hardships as the men as they tried to carve a
life out of the wilderness. They helped build cabins and clear
land for planting. They hauled water from springs, grew cotton
for clothes, and hunted wild animals. Though no early tall tales
celebrate an abiding heroine, the Davy Crockett Almanacks do
present rugged frontier women in a number of vignettes, such
as "Sal Fink, the Mississippi Screamer," "Nance Bowers Taming
a Bear," "Katy Goodgrit and the Wolves," and "Sappina Wing
and the Crocodile." In these stories the Davy Crockett
character tells about comically outrageous women who display
amazing boldness and ingenuity.

In the following tale I have chosen to combine these
various female characters into a single heroine—and have
called her Sally Ann Thunder Ann Whirlwind, the name
of Davy's fictional wife, who is briefly mentioned in the
Davy Crockett Almanacks.

One early spring day, when the leaves of the white oaks were about as big as a mouse's ear, Davy Crockett set out alone through the forest to do some bear hunting. Suddenly it started raining real hard, and he felt obliged to stop for shelter under a tree. As he shook the rain out of his coonskin cap, he got sleepy, so he laid back into the crotch of the tree, and pretty soon he was snoring.

Davy slept so hard, he didn't wake up until nearly sundown. And when he did, he discovered that somehow or another in all that sleeping his head had gotten stuck in the crotch of the tree, and he couldn't get it out.

Well, Davy roared loud enough to make the tree lose all its little mouse-ear leaves. He twisted and turned and carried on for over an hour, but still that tree wouldn't let go. Just as he was about to give himself up for a goner, he heard a girl say, "What's the matter, stranger?"

Even from his awkward position, he could see that she was extraordinary—tall as a hickory sapling, with arms as big as a keelboat tiller's.

"My head's stuck, sweetie," he said. "And if you help me get it free, I'll give you a pretty little comb."

"Don't call me sweetie," she said. "And don't worry about giving me no pretty little comb, neither. I'll free your old coconut, but just because I want to."

Then this extraordinary girl did something that made Davy's hair stand on end. She reached in a bag and took out a bunch of rattlesnakes. She tied all the wriggly critters together to make a long rope, and as she tied, she kept talking. "I'm not a shy little colt," she said. "And I'm not a little singing nightingale, neither. I can tote a steamboat on my back, outscream a panther, and jump over my own shadow. I can double up crocodiles any day, and I like to wear a hornets' nest for my Sunday bonnet."

As the girl looped the ends of her snake rope to the top of the branch that was trapping Davy, she kept bragging: "I'm a streak of lightning set up edgeways and buttered with quicksilver. I can outgrin, outsnort, outrun, outlift, outsneeze, outsleep, outlie any varmint from Maine to Louisiana. Furthermore, *sweetie*, I can blow out the moonlight and sing a wolf to sleep." Then she pulled on the other end of the snake rope so hard, it seemed as if she might tear the world apart.

The right-hand fork of that big tree bent just about double. Then Davy slid his head out as easy as you please. For a minute he was so dizzy, he couldn't tell up from down. But when he got everything going straight again, he took a good look at that girl. "What's your name, ma'am?"

"Sally Ann Thunder Ann Whirlwind," she said. "But if you mind your manners, you can call me Sally."

From then on Davy Crockett was crazy in love with Sally Ann Thunder Ann Whirlwind. He asked everyone he knew about her, and everything he heard caused another one of Cupid's arrows to jab him in the gizzard.

"Oh, I know Sally!" the preacher said. "She can dance a rock to pieces and ride a panther bareback!"

"Sally's a good ole friend of mine," the blacksmith said. "Once I seen her crack a walnut with her front teeth."

"Sally's so very special," said the schoolmarm. "She likes to whip across the Salt River, using her apron for a sail and her left leg for a rudder!"

Sally Ann Thunder Ann Whirlwind had a reputation for being funny, too. Her best friend, Lucy, told Davy, "Sally can laugh the bark off a pine tree. She likes to whistle out one side of her mouth while she eats with the other side and grins with the middle!"

According to her friends, Sally could tame about anything in the world, too. They all told Davy about the time she was churning butter and heard something scratching outside. Suddenly the door swung open, and in walked the Great King Bear of the Mud Forest. He'd come to steal one of her smoked hams. Well, before the King Bear could say boo, Sally grabbed a warm dumpling from the pot and stuffed it in his mouth.

The dumpling tasted so good, the King Bear's eyes winked with tears. But then he started to think that Sally might taste pretty good, too. So opening and closing his big old mouth, he backed her right into a corner.

Sally was plenty scared, with her knees a-knocking and her heart a-hammering. But just as the King Bear blew his hot breath in her face, she gathered the courage to say, "Would you like to dance?"

As everybody knows, no bear can resist an invitation to a square dance, so of course the old fellow forgot all about eating Sally and said, "Love to."

Then he bowed real pretty, and the two got to kicking and whooping and swinging each other through the air, as Sally sang:

> *We are on our way to Baltimore,*
> *With two behind, and two before:*
> *Around, around, around we go,*
> *Where oats, peas, beans, and barley grow!*

And while she was singing, Sally tied a string from the bear's ankle to her butter churn, so that all the time the old feller was kicking up his legs and dancing around the room, he was also churning her butter!

And folks loved to tell the story about Sally's encounter with another stinky varmint—only this one was a *human* varmint. It seems that Mike Fink, the riverboat man, decided to scare the toenails off Sally because he was sick and tired of hearing Davy Crockett talk about how great she was.

One evening Mike crept into an old alligator skin and met Sally just as she was taking off to forage in the woods for berries. He spread open his gigantic mouth and made such a howl that he nearly scared himself to death. But Sally paid no more attention to that fool than she would have to a barking puppy dog.

However, when Mike put out his claws to embrace
her, her anger rose higher than a Mississippi flood. She
threw a flash of eye lightning at him, turning the dark to
daylight. Then she pulled out a little toothpick and with a
single swing sent the alligator head flying fifty feet! And
then to finish him off good, she rolled up her sleeves and
knocked Mike Fink clear across the woods and into a
muddy swamp.

When the fool came to, Davy Crockett was standing over him. "What in the world happened to you, Mikey?" he asked.

"Well, I—I think I must-a been hit by some kind of wild alligator!" Mike stammered, rubbing his sore head.

Davy smiled, knowing full well it was Sally Ann Thunder Ann Whirlwind just finished giving Mike Fink the only punishment he'd ever known.

That incident caused Cupid's final arrow to jab Davy's gizzard. "Sally's the whole steamboat," he said, meaning she was something great. The next day he put on his best raccoon hat and sallied forth to see her.

When he got within three miles of her cabin, he began to holler her name. His voice was so loud, it whirled through the woods like a hurricane.

Sally looked out and saw the wind a-blowing and the trees a-bending. She heard her name a-thundering through the woods, and her heart began to thump. By now she'd begun to feel that Davy Crockett was the whole steamboat, too. So she put on her best hat—an eagle's nest with a wildcat's tail for a feather—and ran outside.

Just as she stepped out the door, Davy Crockett burst from the woods and jumped onto her porch as fast as a frog. "Sally, darlin'!" he cried. "I think my heart is bustin'! Want to be my wife?"

"Oh, my stars and possum dogs, why not?" she said.

From that day on, Davy Crockett had a hard time acting tough around Sally Ann Thunder Ann Whirlwind. His fightin' and hollerin' had no more effect on her than dropping feathers on a barn floor. At least that's what *she'd* tell you. *He* might say something else.

How to
Write a
Funny Poem

There is something about a poem—
a silly, tickle-your-funny-bone,
kick-up-your-feet
kind of poem—that makes
a person grab a pencil and want
to write his or her own.

What is a funny poem? A funny poem
can be rhymed, limericked, rapped,
or have a rhythm all its own.
It can tell a joke, or exaggerate
facts, as long as the end result
makes you laugh.

Oodles of Noodles

I love noodles. Give me oodles.
Make a mound up to the sun.
Noodles are my favorite foodles.
I eat noodles by the ton.

Lucia and James L. Hymes, Jr.

- The subject of the poem can be as silly as you want.

- A poet can create different rhyme patterns. In this poem, lines 1 and 3 have rhymes in them, and lines 2 and 4 rhyme.

A Young Lady of Crete

There was a young lady of Crete,
Who was so exceedingly neat,
When she got out of bed
She stood on her head,
To make sure of not soiling her feet.

Anonymous

- All limericks have the same pattern of rhythm and rhyme.

1 Brainstorm Topics

On your own, brainstorm some funny topics for your poem. Think about jokes and stories you know. Imagine ridiculous situations that could never really happen. And don't forget about everyday situations— even a messy room can be funny if you describe it creatively. (Well, maybe your family wouldn't agree!) Once you have a list of ideas, choose one.

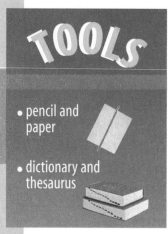

TOOLS

- pencil and paper
- dictionary and thesaurus

2 Pick a Form

Your funny poem can be whatever you want it to be—long or short, a rap or a rhyme, or just a few silly lines. You can write your poem to look like a shape. If your poem is about a bowling ball, try writing it in a circle. If you want to write a limerick, look through poetry books for examples. Think about what you want your poem to say. Then choose the form that you think will work best.

Tip • Try using words that sound funny, such as *boing* or *zing,* or make up words of your own.

3 Write Your Poem

Once you've decided what form you want your poem to take, start writing. When you're finished, read it aloud to yourself. Does it sound flat in places? You may want to change one or two words so that the rhythm is stronger. If you'd like your poem to rhyme (it doesn't have to), here's a hint: Use a rhyming dictionary or a thesaurus to help you find new words.

A hat, it is said, will always have a job. Since it **KNOWS** how to get ahead.

4 Have a Poetry Reading

Have a poetry reading in your classroom. If you prefer, add pictures and make your poem into a greeting card. Send it to a friend who could use a good laugh. You could also combine your poem with others and make a class book.

If You Are Using a Computer . . .

Use the thesaurus on your computer as you write your poem. You can create banners and posters on the computer to advertise your poetry reading.

THINK

How can the rhyme and rhythm of a poem help make it funny?

Robb Armstrong
Cartoonist ▶

People use humor to entertain
each other.

Funny People

Learn how an
illustrator turned
his talent for
doodling into
a career.

Travel back in time to
a prehistoric land.

Cheer for Amy as
she tries to
become a riddle
champion. Then
learn a recipe for
making riddles.

P R O J E C T

Turn a funny situation or joke
into a comic strip.

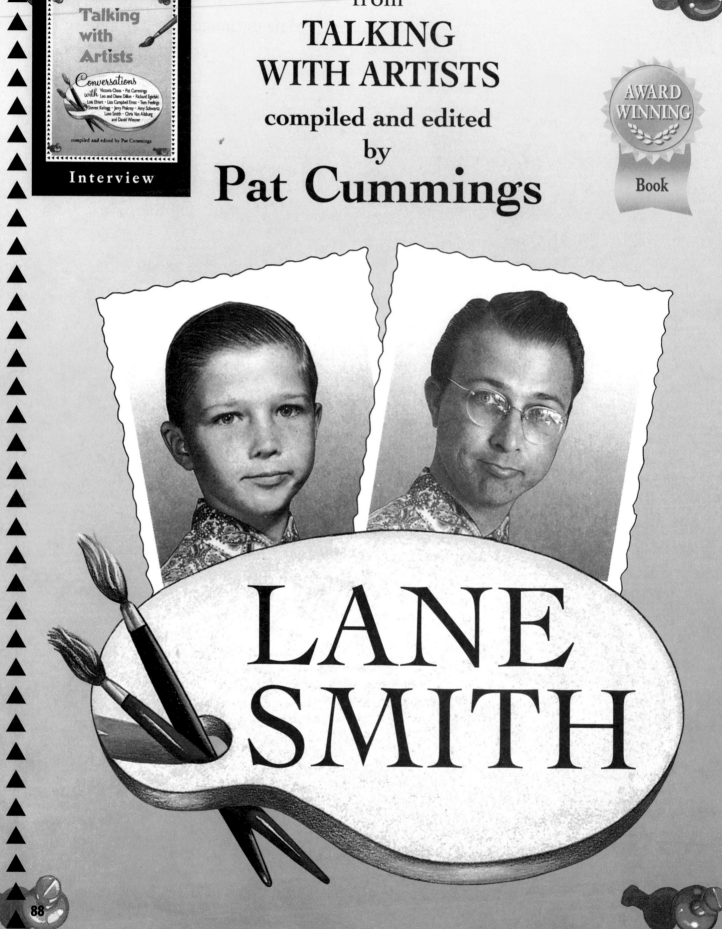

SOURCE

Talking with Artists

Conversations with Leo and Diane Dillon · Richard Egielski
Lois Ehlert · Lisa Campbell Ernst · Tom Feelings
Steven Kellogg · Jerry Pinkney · Amy Schwartz
Lane Smith · Chris Van Allsburg
and David Wiesner

compiled and edited by Pat Cummings

Interview

from
TALKING
WITH ARTISTS
compiled and edited
by
Pat Cummings

AWARD
WINNING

Book

LANE
SMITH

Birthday: August 25, 1959

MY STORY

THE CIRCLE STAGE

I've always doodled and scribbled, but the moment when things really started to click was when I discovered the "Circle Concept." You see, *all* cartoon characters are made up primarily of circles. In fact, a lot of things are. Up until then I just let my pencil wander all over the place, never drawing anything the same way twice. Starting with circles put a little structure into my artwork—and made things a lot easier.

See . . .

Well, the "Circle Concept" worked for *almost* everything.

THE SPACE STAGE

I think one of my fondest memories is of lying stretched out on the library floor at Parkridge Elementary, reading Eleanor Cameron's *Wonderful Flight to the Mushroom Planet.* I loved the story and the art. To this day, whenever I smell hard-boiled eggs I think of how Chuck and David saved the planet with the sulfur-smelling eggs.

From then on I drew only "space stuff."

See . . .

Mr. Space. **Age 8. Pencil and crayon, 5 x 2¾".**

THE OTHER STAGES

Over the years I went through a lot of other stages, too — the CAR AND SUBMARINE STAGE, the BASEBALL STAGE, the SUPERHERO STAGE, the BUG STAGE, and so on.

And each stage had its moments. When I was ten, I made an animated flip-book of a baseball player pitching. When I was fourteen, I sent samples of my superheroes to Marvel Comics and they actually answered back with a letter of encouragement and a free sheet of the official art board that their artists used (Wow! Free paper!).

For a while I was into trees. By the way, have you ever noticed that all trees drawn by kids must have this thing on them? We don't know what makes us draw it, or even what it is, for that matter—it's just something we're born with.

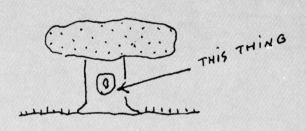

THIS THING

In junior high and high school I received a lot of encouragement from my art teachers. My junior high teacher, Ms. Ng, entered some of my work in an art show and it actually won!!!*

Then in high school, Mr. Baughman convinced me to experiment with different types of materials. I tried acrylics, oil paints, pen and ink, and watercolor. I learned that different media could create different moods (watercolors make great sad-rainy-day pictures).

Mr. Baughman also exposed me to all kinds of art and illustration in books. When I finally did my own book, *Flying Jake*, I dedicated it to him.

I am glad things worked out the way they did and I am able to spend my life drawing pictures for a living. I can't imagine what would've happened if I had decided to become a mathematician.

* "Honorable Mention"

"TO BE AN ARTIST YOU HAVE TO KEEP ON DOING ART—JUST DRAW, DRAW, DRAW!"—LANE SMITH

1. Where do you get your ideas from?

I get my ideas from everything! Like the way somebody parts their hair might give me an idea for a picture of a winding river, or shoestrings in knots can inspire drawings of futuristic highways. Of course if that doesn't work, I just copy the drawings from my comic books.

2. Do you have any children? Any pets?

Yes, I have one child. His name is A.J. He is a cat. He is fat.

3. What do you enjoy drawing the most?

Faces.

4. Do you ever put people you know in your pictures?

Not directly, but elements of them creep into my work, and that big, fat cat in *The Big Pets* looks very familiar.

5. What do you use to make your pictures?

Oil paints, and sometimes I add (collage) real things into my illustrations like sticks, old photos, newspaper clippings, and so on.

I did a book with Jon Scieszka called *The True Story of the Three Little Pigs!* I collaged a bunch of stuff into that one. Jon said, "How creative!" Little did he know it was really saving me a lot of painting time.

Heh, heh.

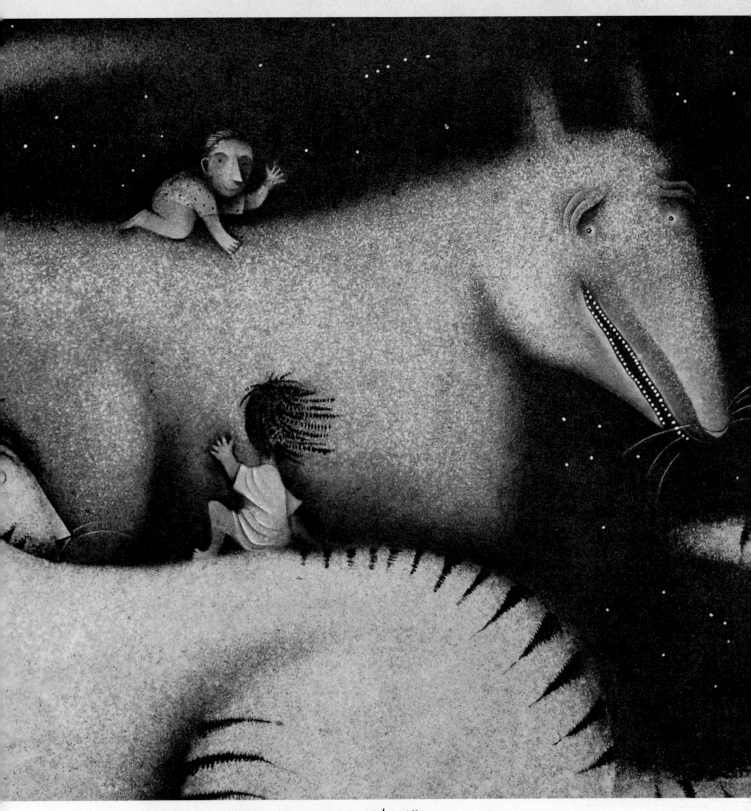

The Big Pets. 1991. Oil painting, 12½ x 9".
Published by Viking Penguin.

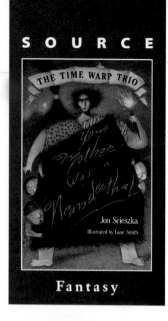

Your Mother Was a Neanderthal

BY JON SCIESZKA
ILLUSTRATED BY LANE SMITH

In Jon Scieszka's The Time Warp Trio series, Fred, Sam, and Joe travel back in time and have many comical adventures. This trip finds the three boys in the Stone Age, where they've met a caveman named Duh and his band of hunters. Now the boys are about to meet somebody new.

Trees shook.

Rocks crashed.

The ground wiggled and suddenly split open right behind us.

The cavemen's logpile home fell into the cracked earth and disappeared. Then everything stopped. No birds, no bugs, no prehistoric beasts made a sound.

I sat up and dusted off my animal skin. "That could have been . . . I mean, that was almost . . . we were almost . . ."

"Smashed into little bits and buried under a ton of prehistoric garbage!" screamed Sam.

"Calm down, Sam," said Fred. "Things could be worse."

"Oh yeah? How?" said Sam, looking a little wild-eyed and crazy. "We're trapped 40,000 years in the past. Everything we meet tries to eat us. And now even the ground underneath us is falling apart. And you say things could be worse? How could things be worse?" Sam smacked himself on the forehead with the palm of his hand.

Duh and his men stood up carefully and moved to the edge of the new ravine. They looked down at the pile of broken logs at the bottom. They looked at Sam. Duh let out a wild yell, then smacked himself in the head. And all at once, all of the guys started yelling, moaning, and smacking their heads.

"That's how," said Fred.

Sam yelled. The caveguys yelled. Sam moaned. The caveguys moaned.

"And how," I said.

The noise of Sam, Duh, and the caveguys grew louder and louder, and suddenly *much* louder.

Duh stopped beating himself up, listened, and then yelled something that sounded like "Woo Maa! Woo Maa!" Everyone ran for the trees and left Fred, Sam, and me staring at each other.

"Woo Maa?" said Fred. "What's Woo Maa?"

Sam stood frozen, looking off into the space over our heads.

"I don't know," I said. "But I think we've lost Sam."

Sam croaked, "Woo . . . woo . . . woo . . . ma . . . ma . . . ma—"

"We've definitely lost him," said Fred.

Sam raised his arm to point and croaked again, "Oh, no. Woolly mammoth!"

"He's snapped. He thinks we're the cavewomen," I said. "It's okay, Sam. It's me, Joe."

And right then I was stopped by an earpopping trumpeted blast of noise. Fred and I turned to look behind us. There, standing at the edge of the clearing, not twenty feet away from us, stood the largest and most crazed-looking beast you will never want to see as long as you live. You've seen them in books. And you've seen their relatives in zoos. And I'm telling you, you don't need to see them any closer.

"Oh, no," I said.

"*Woolly mammoth!*" yelled Fred.

At that moment I understood where the word *mammoth* came from. This thing was huge. It was gigantic. Enormous. Mammoth.

The mammoth jerked his head back and fixed us with one tiny eye. Fortunately, he seemed just as surprised to see us as we were to see him. Unfortunately, he stood about ten feet taller and weighed about two tons more than us. And most unfortunately, we were standing in his way.

We stood face to face, not knowing what to do. Fred bent down slowly and picked up a stick that had broken off to a point.

"Our only chance is to scare him off."

"Let's not do anything that might make him mad," I whispered.

"We could turn and run," said Fred.

Sam inched backward. "That sounds good to me."

"But we'd probably get trampled from behind."

"That doesn't sound so good to me."

Fred eyed the huge, hairy ancestor of an elephant in front of us. He raised his stick and then threw it as hard as he could. The makeshift spear sailed through the air and struck the mammoth right between the eyes.

The mammoth blinked and slowly shook its gigantic head and pointy tusks. Fred's spear fell to the ground like a used toothpick. The mammoth lowered those pointy tusks in our direction and trumpeted.

"Time for another disappearing act," I said. "Because now I think you made him mad."

The hairy monster shook its mammoth head again and raised one mammoth foot.

And that's the last thing I saw because we turned and ran for the trees. We dodged around bushes and rocks. The mammoth smashed through the bushes and rocks. We were running as fast as we could, but the mammoth was still gaining on us and there was nowhere to hide.

We ran. Mammoth footsteps shook the ground behind us. We ran. Hot, smelly, mammoth breath blasted the back of my neck. I knew we were goners. But I wondered if our math teacher would believe the note from home: "Dear Mr. Dexter, Please excuse Joe, Sam, and Fred for not doing their math homework. They got run over by a woolly mammoth."

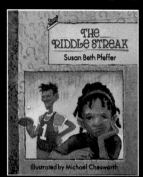

FROM THE
RIDDLE

by Susan Beth Pfeffer

illustrated by Tyrone Geter

STREAK

Just once, Amy would like to be better at something than her older brother Peter. He wins every game they play, and he seems to have an answer for every question. Out of desperation, she decides to become a riddle expert. After all, Peter can't know the answer to every riddle.

Amy sat next to Maria on the school bus Monday morning. "How many riddles does your grandfather know?" she asked.

"Millions," Maria said.

"I mean it," Amy said. "How many riddles?"

"I don't know," Maria said. "Lots and lots. Why?"

"Do you think he could teach me some?" Amy asked.

"Sure," Maria said. "Why do you need to know riddles?"

"To beat my big brother," Amy said.

"I wish I had a big brother," Maria said. "All I have are two little sisters. They drive me crazy."

"I'll trade you," Amy said. "One big brother for two little sisters and a grandfather who knows riddles. Do you think we could go visit him after school?"

"No," Maria said.

"Tomorrow then?" Amy asked. She didn't know how long she could wait before finding a riddle Peter didn't know.

"My grandparents went down to Florida this weekend," Maria said. "They won't be back until April."

"But that's months from now," Amy said. "I need a riddle right away."

"Try the library," Maria said. "Ms. Morris knows lots of good stuff."

Amy waited impatiently until the bus finally pulled into the school. As soon as she got off, she ran to the library. There were still a few minutes before the first bell was going to ring.

"Do you know any riddles?" she asked Ms. Morris.

"What kind of riddles?" Ms. Morris asked.

"Any kind," Amy said. "Hard ones."

"How many do you need?" Ms. Morris said.

"I don't know," Amy said. "I need a riddle my brother doesn't know."

"Oh dear," Ms. Morris said. "I remember Peter when he was at the primary school. He knew lots of riddles."

"Do you remember them all?" Amy asked. "If I know all the riddles he knows, then I could maybe find one he doesn't."

"Wait a second," Ms. Morris said. "I think there might be an easier approach."

"What?" Amy asked. She had nothing against easy.

"I just got in a brand-new riddle book last week," Ms. Morris said. "Peter might know some of the riddles in it, but there have got to be a few he doesn't know yet. Let me show you the book." She looked under her desk and pulled the book out. "Here it is," she said. "*The Riddle Encyclopedia*. That sounds pretty impressive."

It was a big book and there were riddles on every page. "Can I take it out?" Amy asked.

"I don't see why not," Ms. Morris said. "You'll be the first person to take this book out. That's always an honor."

Amy didn't feel nearly as honored as she did relieved. With an entire brand-new book devoted to riddles, she was bound to come up with one Peter had never heard of.

Amy spent every spare minute at school that day copying out riddles from *The Riddle Encyclopedia*. By the time the school bus arrived at her house, she had twenty riddles carefully written out.

It was wonderful picturing Peter not knowing the answers to any of them. She could see him stammer and stumble and finally cry as riddle after riddle went unanswered. Amy wanted a riddle streak of at least ten, but fifteen, or better still, twenty seemed really perfect to her. She'd earned her streak honestly, by going to the library and doing work. It had nothing to do with being older or bigger. Those kinds of streaks didn't mean anything.

She went crazy waiting for Peter to arrive home from school. Her mother was already there, but she was working in her home office, so Amy didn't feel she could interrupt. Besides, she'd certainly find out about it at suppertime, when Peter would still be crying.

Amy waited in the kitchen, writing out a couple more riddles. There was nothing wrong with a twenty-two riddle streak, or a twenty-five one. She wondered if Peter would ever stop sobbing. She kind of hoped not.

"I'm home!" Peter shouted when he finally got in.

"Mom's working," Amy said. "Don't shout."

"I'm home," Peter whispered instead, and then he laughed. Amy laughed too. It was probably the last time Peter would laugh in his lifetime. "Want some milk?" he asked Amy.

"I had some already," Amy said. She watched as Peter poured himself a glass. "Where do cars get the most flat tires?" she asked. She'd take him by surprise.

"At the fork in the road," Peter said. "Is there any cake left?"

"I don't know," Amy said. It was a good thing she had a few spare riddles to get her streak going. "There are cookies."

"Then I'll have them instead," Peter said.

"What goes out black and comes back white?" Amy asked.

"A cow in a snowstorm," Peter said. "No chocolate chip cookies, huh."

"Dad ate the last one yesterday," Amy said. "There are Fig Newtons left."

"I'd rather have chocolate chip," Peter said, but he took three Fig Newtons anyway.

"Why did the kid put his head on the piano?" Amy asked.

"Because he wanted to play by ear," Peter said. "Next?"

"What kind of doctor treats ducks?"

"A quack," Peter said.

Amy looked down at her list. Peter's riddle streak was definitely doing better than her own. It was a good thing she had a long list.

"What do brave soldiers eat?" she asked.

"Hero sandwiches," Peter said.

"What kind of cat works for the Red Cross?" Amy asked.

"A first-aid kit," Peter said. He rammed a Fig Newton into his mouth, then took a big gulp of milk.

"What pet is always found on the floor?" Amy asked.

"A carpet," Peter said. "Don't you know any hard ones?"

"I know lots of hard ones," Amy said. She searched her list frantically, looking for some hard ones. She was starting to feel really nervous. "What kind of house weighs the least?"

"A lighthouse," Peter said. He ate another of the Fig Newtons. "Are you sure there aren't any chocolate chip cookies left?"

"Why did the robber take a bath?" Amy asked.

"So he could make a clean getaway," Peter said. "What did you do, study riddles at school today?"

"I know lots of riddles you don't know," Amy said.

"Sure," Peter said. "And you can beat me in Ping-Pong any time you want."

"What travels around the world but stays in one corner?" Amy asked.

"A stamp," Peter said. "Do I get to ask you any riddles?"

"No," Amy said.

"That's a shame," Peter said. "Because I took out this really good riddle book from my library last week. It's called *The Riddle Encyclopedia*, and it had lots of riddles I never knew before."

"You already read *The Riddle Encyclopedia*?" Amy asked.

"Sure," Peter said. "My librarian showed it to me as soon as it came into the library. I read it on Saturday when you wouldn't play with me. Are you sure there aren't any chocolate chip cookies left?"

"I'm positive!" Amy shouted. She ran out of the kitchen and to her bedroom, leaving Peter behind with her list of foolproof riddles.

"**W**e're certainly quiet tonight," Mr. Gale said that evening as they finished supper. "Is there a reason why none of us is talking?"

"My mind's on work," Mrs. Gale admitted. "I'm sorry."

"I suppose your mind is on school," Mr. Gale said to Peter.

"No," Peter said. "I just don't have anything to say."

"What about you, Amy?" Mr. Gale asked. "Didn't anything interesting happen to you today?"

"No," Amy said. She certainly wasn't going to tell her father she'd spent the whole day learning riddles Peter already knew.

"In that case, how about dessert?" Mr. Gale asked. "I don't suppose there's any cake left?"

"We finished it last night," Mrs. Gale said.

"I was afraid of that," Mr. Gale said. "You know, I've been thinking about that cake all day long."

"It was good," Mrs. Gale said. "Sometimes I think cake-mix cakes are better than the ones you bake from scratch."

"What did the baseball say to the cake mix?" Amy asked.

"What?" Mr. Gale said.

"It's a riddle," Amy said. "What did the baseball say to the cake mix?"

"Nothing," Peter said. "Baseballs can't talk."

"They can in riddles," Amy said.

"This is a good riddle," Mrs. Gale said. "What did the baseball say to the cake mix? I don't know that one."

"Neither do I," Mr. Gale said. "How about it, Peter? You're the riddle king around here."

"Baseball," Peter said. "Cake mix. I don't remember that one from *The Riddle Encyclopedia*."

"Give up?" Amy asked.

"One more second," Peter said. "I must know it from somewhere. I know every riddle ever invented."

"I bet you don't know this one," Amy said. "Oh, I'm sorry, Mom, about betting."

"Don't be," her mother said. "I bet Peter doesn't know either."

"Do you, Peter?" Mr. Gale asked.

"I must," Peter said. "There can't be a riddle Amy knows and I don't."

"Your time is up," Mrs. Gale said. "I want to know the answer. Amy, what did the baseball say to the cake mix?"

"Batter up!" Amy said.

Everyone laughed. Except Peter.

"I never heard that one before," Peter said. "Where did you learn it?"

"I made it up," Amy said. "Just now, when Mom was talking about cake mixes."

"Did you really?" her father said. "I don't think I ever heard a brand-new riddle before. Peter, have you ever made up any riddles?"

"No," Peter said. "I never thought I needed to. There are millions of riddles already."

"Well, now there are millions and one," Mrs. Gale said. "Amy, that's wonderful, making up a riddle like that."

"I just thought of another one," Amy said. "Knock knock."

"Who's there?" Peter asked.

"Batter," Amy said.

"Batter who?" Peter asked.

"I'm batter than you are!" Amy sang in triumph.

Amy's parents laughed. "She got you on that one," Amy's father said to Peter.

"That's not fair!" Peter said.

"Why not?" his mother asked.

"I don't know," he admitted. "But it isn't."

"I have another one!" Amy said.

"You're kidding," her father said. "Amy, this is quite a riddle streak."

"What did Porky Pig say to the silverware?" Amy asked.

Her mother, father, and brother all stared at her. It was possibly the best moment in Amy's life.

"Th . . . th . . . th . . . that's all, forks!" Amy shouted.

Everyone, even Peter, laughed. "I've got to write these down," her father said. "I'll show them off at work tomorrow."

"Me too," Peter said.

"What do you mean?" Amy asked.

"Remember that guy, Mike Rudolph?" Peter asked. "The one who beats me in everything? He knows every riddle in the book. That's why I memorized them, to beat him at riddles, but it didn't work. Tomorrow I'll try Amy's riddles on him. He's bound not to know them. It'll drive him crazy."

"You'd better tell him they're mine," Amy said.

"I sure will," Peter said. "When he hears some dumb, I mean, smart little third grader made them up, he'll really go nuts."

"You want me to make up some more?" Amy asked.

"I sure do," Peter said. "After dessert, let's go to my room and I'll write them all down."

"Amy Gale, Riddle Champ!" her mother said. "Three brand-new riddles and still going strong."

It was definitely the best moment in Amy Gale's life.

SOURCE

STORYWORKS
FACT · FICTION · FUN

Magazine

The Riddle King's Riddle Recipe!

By Mike Thaler
Illustrated by Jared Lee

WHO HAM I?

PIG

My name is Mike Thaler. They call me America's Riddle King! This is my riddle recipe. Use it to create millions of your own original riddles on any subject.

1. Pick a subject:

PIG

2. Make a list of synonyms and related words:

HOG, SWINE, OINK, HAM, MUD, SNOUT

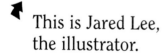

This is Jared Lee, the illustrator.

If you follow this simple recipe you can soon be a Riddle King or Riddle Queen!

So oinkers away! Have fun, happy riddling, and never forget: The most powerful nation in the world is your imagi-nation!

HINT: A thesaurus, an encyclopedia, or a book about your subject can help you find words related to your subject.

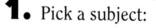

AWARD WINNING

Magazine

3. Take any word from the list: **HAM**

Drop off the first letter, leaving: **AM**

4. List words that begin with **AM**:
AMBULANCE, AMNESIA

5. Put the **H** back on:
HAMBULANCE, HAMNESIA

These are your riddle answers.

6. Now make up your riddle question using the answer's definition:

HOW DO YOU TAKE A PIG TO THE HOSPITAL?
Answer:
IN A HAMBULANCE

WHAT DO YOU CALL IT WHEN A PIG LOSES ITS MEMORY?
Answer:
HAMNESIA

HINT: In some cases, you have to drop off more than one letter to get a good word to work with. For example:

SNOUT – SN = OUT

OUTFIELDER + SN = SNOUTFIELDER
(What position does a pig play on a baseball team?)

OUTERSPACE + SN = SNOUTER SPACE
(Where do pig astronauts travel?)

How to
Create a Comic Strip

With a *pen* and a *joke*, you can make your own *comic strip*.

What's the funniest part of the newspaper? Many people would answer, the comics. A comic strip is a story told with words and pictures. Some comic strips can be about serious subjects, even when they are funny. The words and pictures are in frames, and the last frame is the punch line—the thing that makes us laugh. Often the pictures make us laugh before we even get to the punch line.

GET UP, CALVIN! I'M NOT GOING TO CALL YOU AGAIN!

YOU DON'T KNOW THE ANSWER? THEN SIT DOWN.

STOP STALLI, AND GET IN BATHTUB.

...SIGHHH

CRAS

1 Brainstorm Ideas

Come up with a list of funny ideas for your comic strip. Include jokes, stories, and funny things that have happened to you. Check your source materials for ideas. When you've finished your list, choose one idea to use for your comic strip. What makes your idea funny? Why does it make you laugh? Can you make a joke out of it? What kind of characters will you use to tell the joke?

TOOLS

- paper, pencil, and ruler
- colored pencils, markers
- joke books, magazines, comic strips

2 Plan Your Comic Strip

After you've picked an idea from your list, think about how to arrange your comic strip. Here are the steps.

Write the Dialogue: Write out the joke. Decide which character will say which lines. Then rewrite the joke using the fewest words possible.

Set Up Your Strip: Before you draw the final version of your strip, sketch out the words and pictures in a diagram like the one shown here. Write the words. Then sketch the characters into the frames. Next, draw speech balloons around the words. Be sure the reader can tell which character is speaking.

How Am I Doing?

Before you create your comic strip, take a few minutes to ask yourself these questions.

- Did I pick a funny joke or idea?
- Did I think about dialogue and pictures for my strip?
- What kind of characters will I draw?

PANEL 1
The characters

PANEL 2
Set up the joke.

PANEL 3
Add to the joke.

PANEL 4
Give the punch line.

117

3 Add Finishing Touches

Jazz up the joke. Next you're ready to create the final version of your comic strip. Look over the sketches and words on your strip. Do you think the joke is funny? Do the expressions on your characters' faces match their words? If you need to make changes, now is a good time.

Pictures make the joke seem funnier. Turn your sketches into really cool art. Use your art supplies and your imagination. Try making practice sketches with colored pencils and then with markers, to see which you prefer.

Create a background for your characters. Do your characters live in the woods? Are they standing on a city street? Think about what kind of background will help make your words even funnier.

 Tips
- Use words like *zap* and *pow* to indicate sound effects.
- If you don't want to draw your characters, think about cutting out figures from magazines and newspapers.
- Use lots of bright colors.

4 Publish Your Comic Strip

When everyone's finished, put all the strips together to create giant newspaper "funny pages." Or you could bind the strips together to make a book. You could also submit your comic strip to the school newspaper.

CRASH

If You Are Using a Computer ...

Make a comic strip using your Card format. Begin your strip on the front, have one or two panels on the inside, and use the back for your punch line. Use the clip art, drawing tools, and speech balloons to make your strip look great.

CONGRATULATIONS

You've learned many ways that humor is used to make people laugh. Remember, a laugh a day is good for everyone.

Robb Armstrong
Cartoonist ▶

Glossary

an·i·mat·ed
(an′ə mā′tid) *adjective*
Having movement or action, such as cartoon characters. He saw the *animated* version of *The Three Little Pigs.*

art·work
(ärt′wûrk′) *noun*
Painting, drawing, or sculpture. She showed me her *artwork.*

bab·bling
(ba′ blēng) *verb*
Making sounds that have no meaning. The baby started *babbling* in his crib. ▲ **babble**

be·seech·ing·ly
(bi sēch′ ing lē) *adverb*
In a way that asks or pleads for something. He looked at his father *beseechingly.*

boomed (bo͞omd) *verb*
Made a loud, deep sound. His voice *boomed* over the loudspeaker.
▲ **boom**

ca·reer (kə rēr′) *noun*
A profession or an occupation that a person has through life.
She chose social work as a *career.*

car·toon char·ac·ters
(kär to͞on′ kar′ ik tərz) *noun*
People or animals that are humorously drawn.
▲ **cartoon character**

col·lage (kə läzh′) *noun*
A picture made by gluing different kinds of materials to a surface.

com·pet·i·tive
(kəm pet′ i tiv) *adjective*
Involving competition; working against others for the same prize or goal. She was very *competitive*, and wanted to win the game.

Word History

The word **competitive** comes from the Latin word, *competere*, meaning "to meet." A meeting between athletes, such as a sports event, is a **competition**.

cre•a•tive
(krē ā′ tiv) *adjective*
Having and showing artistic abilities and imagination. His robot sculptures are very *creative*.

Thesaurus

creative

artistic
inventive
original

cried (krīd) *verb*
Called out in surprise.
▲ **cry**

dead•line
(ded′ līn) *noun*
The latest time by which something has to be completed. The *deadline* for handing in her report is Friday.

de•vel•op•ment
(di vel′ əp ment) *noun*
The act of creating something new. He worked on the *development* of a new product.

doo•dled
(dood′ ld) *verb*
Scribbled or drew things without paying attention. She *doodled* on the paper while talking on the phone. ▲ **doodle**

en•cy•clo•pe•di•a
(en sī′ klə pē′ dē ə) *noun*
A book or set of books containing information arranged alphabetically on many different subjects.

fic•tion•al
(fik′ shə nl) *adjective*
Anything made up or imagined. The giant jackalope is a *fictional* animal.

fraz•zled
(fraz′ əld) *adjective*
To be emotionally or physically worn out. He looked old and *frazzled*.

a	add	o͝o	took	ə =
ā	ace	o͞o	pool	a in *above*
â	care	u	up	e in *sicken*
ä	palm	û	burn	i in *possible*
e	end	yo͞o	fuse	o in *melon*
ē	equal	oi	oil	u in *circus*
i	it	ou	pout	
ī	ice	ng	ring	
o	odd	th	thin	
ō	open	th	this	
ô	order	zh	vision	

Glossary

fron·tier
(frun tēr´) *noun*
The farthest settlement that lies next to an unexplored region. She had a hard life living on the *frontier.*

her·o·ine
(her´ ō in) *noun*
A woman admired for her bravery and courage. In the movie, the *heroine* saved the town.

hol·lered
(hol´ ərd) *verb*
Shouted or called loudly. He *hollered* for the dogs to come back. ▲ **holler**

il·lus·tra·tion
(il´ə strā´ shən) *noun*
A picture or diagram used to decorate or explain something. The poster *illustration* was beautiful.

im·ag·i·na·tion
(i maj´ ə nā´ shən) *noun*
The ability to form pictures in the mind; creative ability.

in·ci·dent
(in´ si dənt) *noun*
An event; something that happens. She described the funny *incident* to the class.

in·dig·nant·ly
(in dig´ nənt lē) *adverb*
In a way that expresses anger or scorn. The man spoke *indignantly* to the rude waiter.

me·di·a
(mē´ dē ə) *noun*
Materials used to create art. She tried many different *media* before deciding on oil paints. ▲ **medium**

mum·bling
(mum´ bling) *verb*
Speaking in such a low voice that the words are not understood. He was *mumbling* to himself. ▲ **mumble**

frontier

or·gan·ized
(ôr´ gə nīzd´) *adjective*
Arranged in an orderly way. She needed to be *organized* to do the experiment.

rep·u·ta·tion
(rep´ yə tā´ shən) *noun*
The character or quality of someone or something as judged by others. He had a *reputation* for being a good teacher.

Thesaurus

reputation
character
fame
status

re·sign·ed·ly
(ri zīn´əd lē) *adverb*
To accept something without really wanting to. When the bell rang, he *resignedly* handed in his test.

rid·dle (rid´ l) *noun*
A question or a problem that requires clever thinking to answer it.

self-dis·ci·plined
(self´ dis´ə plind) *adjective*
Controlling oneself. A writer needs to be *self-disciplined*.

shrieked (shrēkt) *verb*
Made a loud, shrill cry.
▲ **shriek**

slurp·ing
(slûrp´ ing) *verb*
Making a loud sipping sound; drinking noisily. The boy was *slurping* juice through his straw.
▲ **slurp**

speech·less
(spēch´ lis) *adjective*
Unable to speak for a moment. When he saw the present, he was *speechless*.

syn·o·nyms
(sin´ ə nimz) *noun*
Words that have similar meanings. Happy and glad are *synonyms* for cheerful. ▲ **synonym**

the·sau·rus
(thi sôr´ əs) *noun*
A dictionary of synonyms.

Word History

The word **thesaurus** comes from a Greek word that means "treasury." In the nineteenth century, it came to mean a book containing a treasury of words, specifically synonyms.

var·mint
(vär´ mənt) *noun*
A person or animal that is considered troublesome. The rat is a mean *varmint*.

Word History

Varmint comes from the word *vermin*, which is from the Latin word *vermis*, meaning "worm." Later, it came to be used for any unwanted animals, such as rats or fleas.

a	add	o͝o	took	ə =
ā	ace	o͞o	pool	a in *above*
â	care	u	up	e in *sicken*
ä	palm	û	burn	i in *possible*
e	end	yo͞o	fuse	o in *melon*
ē	equal	oi	oil	u in *circus*
i	it	ou	pout	
ī	ice	ng	ring	
o	odd	th	thin	
ō	open	th	this	
ô	order	zh	vision	

Authors & Illustrators

Judy Blume *pages 10–25*
Before starting a new book, this popular author fills a notebook with story details, including scraps of dialogue and other things she does not want to forget. Then she writes and rewrites. Most of her books take her more than a year to complete!

Tyrone Geter *pages 100–111*
Tyrone Geter has traveled to western Africa and has taught art at a university in Nigeria. Today he lives in Akron, Ohio, with his wife. He loves to illustrate books and is always busy with a new project. He also loves to teach. He divides his time between working on his own art and teaching art at the University of Akron.

Mary Pope Osborne *pages 72–81*

This author had a lot of jobs before she wrote her first book at age 30. She traveled around the world; worked as a window dresser, a waitress, and a medical assistant. But once she wrote a book, she finally knew what she really wanted to be: an author. Over the next 10 years, she wrote 20 books!

Tony Ross *pages 32–39*

The first drawings this illustrator created were cartoons for magazines. While trying to illustrate his first book for young readers, his editor told him the art was too stiff. The editor suggested he should draw the art like he drew his cartoons. Since then, Tony Ross has always had fun with his drawings.

Jon Scieszka *pages 94–99*

This author loves to have fun. His first book turned the well-known story about the Three Little Pigs upside-down: his version is told by the Big Bad Wolf! John Sciezka tests his story ideas on his own two kids, Casey and Jake, who make sure the stories are silly enough. They usually are! By the way, the author's last name is pronounced: sheh•ska.

"I get most of my ideas from hanging out with kids."

Books &

Author Study

More by Jack Prelutsky

**A. Nonny Mouse
Writes Again**
*illustrated by Marjorie
Priceman*
Here are more poems by
one of history's greatest
poets.

The New Kid on the Block
*illustrated by James
Stevenson*
This collection is full of
poems about all kinds of
humorous situations.

Tyrannosaurus Was a Beast
illustrated by Arnold Lobel
This collection of funny
poems includes lots of
facts about dinosaurs.

Fiction

**The Knee-High Man and
Other Stories**
by Julius Lester
This collection of
folk tales comes from the
African-American
tradition. The tales are
full of humor, trickery,
and surprises.

Stage Fright
by Ann M. Martin
Sara Holland is the
shyest girl in fourth
grade. Now she has the
leading role in the class
play! This funny book
tells about everything
Sara goes through
as she gets ready to be
a star.

Wanted...Mud Blossom
by Betsy Byars
One of the funniest
families in fiction
searches for truth,
justice, and their dog.

Nonfiction

Funny You Should Ask
*by Marvin Terban
illustrated by John O'Brien*
This book shows you
how to create jokes and
riddles by playing with
words and their
meanings. Get ready to
make people laugh!

**The Young Cartoonist:
The ABCs of Cartooning**
by Syd Hoff
This book is for kids
who are just learning to
draw cartoons. It has
hundreds of illustrations,
plus step-by-step
instructions to help the
beginner achieve results
quickly.

Media

Videos

Be a Cartoonist
Mid Com
Could you really draw your own cartoons? Professional cartoonist Alan Silberberg thinks so. He hosts this how-to video and explains the secrets of his craft. (60 minutes)

The Clown
Public Media Video
A homeless boy dreams of becoming a circus performer. One day he meets an old man who was once a clown. As their relationship grows and his respect for the elderly man increases, the boy finds a way to make his dream come true. (54 minutes)

Software

Cartoonin'.
Remarkable
(IBM)
Create your own comic strip with the help of this program. It includes a drawing editor, story editor, and sound effects.

Print Shop Deluxe, Comic Characters Graphics
Broderbund (MAC)
This special add-on to a popular program gives you lots of graphics options to help you create your own comic strip.

Quicktoons
Wayzata (Macintosh with CD-ROM, IBM-Windows)
Enjoy classic cartoons on your computer with this resource.

Magazines

Cricket
Open Court
This magazine is full of all kinds of stories and articles. The cartoon adventures of Cricket and his friends run throughout each magazine, adding humor to every possible situation.

A Place to Write

Clowns of America, P.O. Box 570, Lake Jackson, TX 77566.

Clowns represent a classic form of comedy. Though it looks like a lot of fun, clowning around can be hard work. If you're interested in how to train to be a clown, you can write to Clowns of America.

Acknowledgments

Grateful acknowledgment is made to the following sources for permission to reprint from previously published material. The publisher has made diligent efforts to trace the ownership of all copyrighted material in this volume and believes that all necessary permissions have been secured. If any errors or omissions have inadvertently been made, proper corrections will gladly be made in future editions.

Cover: Peter Spacek.

Interior: "Mr. and Mrs. Juicy-O" from TALES OF A FOURTH GRADE NOTHING by Judy Blume. Copyright © 1972 by Judy Blume. Cover illustration copyright © 1972 by E. P. Dutton. Used by permission of Dutton Children's Books, a division of Penguin Books USA Inc.

"Laughing Is Good for You" by Karen Burns from *Scholastic News*, April 30, 1993. Text and illustrations copyright © 1993 by Scholastic Inc. Reprinted by permission of Scholastic Inc.

JUMP START by Robb Armstrong. Copyright © 1994 by United Features Syndicate, Inc. Reprinted by permission of United Features Syndicate, Inc.

"Earth Hounds" from EARTH HOUNDS AS EXPLAINED BY PROFESSOR XARGLE by Jeanne Willis, illustrated by Tony Ross. Copyright © 1989 by Jeanne Willis and Tony Ross. Used by permission of Dutton Signet, a division of Penguin Books USA Inc. and Andersen Press Limited, UK, for Canadian rights.

Selection from PRINCE CINDERS by Babette Cole. Copyright © 1988 by Babette Cole. Reprinted by permission of G. P. Putnam's Sons and Hamish Hamilton Ltd. Cover from GRIMMS' FAIRY TALES. Illustrations by Fritz Kredel. Copyright © 1945, renewed 1973 by Grosset & Dunlap, Inc. Reprinted by permission of Grosset & Dunlap, Inc.

Selection from television script adaptation of THE HOBOKEN CHICKEN EMERGENCY. Script adaptation by Arthur Alsberg and Don Nelson. Copyright © 1984. Based on the novel by D. Manus Pinkwater. Reprinted by permission of Arthur Alsberg and Don Nelson.

Poems, illustrations, and cover from POEMS OF A. NONNY MOUSE, compiled by Jack Prelutsky. Compilation copyright © 1989 by Jack Prelutsky. Illustrations copyright © 1989 by Henrik Drescher. Reprinted by arrangement with Alfred A. Knopf, Inc.

"The Talking Mule" from MULES AND MEN by Zora Neale Hurston. Copyright © 1935 by Zora Neale Hurston. Copyright © renewed 1963 by John C. Hurston and Joel Hurston. Reprinted by permission of HarperCollins Publishers. Book cover from FROM SEA TO SHINING SEA, edited by Amy L. Cohn. Copyright

© 1993 by Scholastic Inc. Illustrations by Donald Crews, copyright © 1993 by Donald Crews. Reprinted by permission.

"Sally Ann Thunder Ann Whirlwind" and cover from AMERICAN TALL TALES by Mary Pope Osborne, illustrated by Michael McCurdy. Text copyright © 1991 by Mary Pope Osborne. Illustrations copyright © 1991 by Michael McCurdy. Reprinted by permission of Alfred A. Knopf, Inc.

"Oodles of Noodles" from OODLES OF NOODLES (p. 83) by Lucia and James L. Hymes, Jr. Copyright © 1964 by Lucia and James L. Hymes, Jr. Reprinted by permission of Addison-Wesley Publishing Company, Inc.

"Conversation with Lane Smith" from TALKING WITH ARTISTS, compiled and edited by Pat Cummings. Copyright © 1992 by Lane Smith. Reprinted by permission of Lane Smith. Cover illustration copyright © 1992 by Pat Cummings. This edition is reprinted by arrangement with Simon & Schuster Books for Young Readers, Simon & Schuster Children's Publishing Division.

Selection and cover from YOUR MOTHER WAS A NEANDERTHAL by Jon Scieszka, illustrated by Lane Smith. Copyright © 1993 by Jon Scieszka. Illustrations copyright © 1993 by Lane Smith. Used by permission of Viking Penguin, a division of Penguin Books USA Inc.

Selection and cover from THE RIDDLE STREAK by Susan Beth Pfeffer. Text copyright © 1993 by Susan Beth Pfeffer. Cover illustration copyright © 1993 by Michael Chesworth. Reprinted by permission of Henry Holt & Co., Inc.

"The Riddle King's Riddle Recipe!" by Mike Thaler. Copyright © 1993 by Mike Thaler. First published in *Storyworks*, September 1993. Reprinted by permission of Mike Thaler and Andrea Brown Literary Agency, Inc.

Comic strip from the INDISPENSABLE CALVIN AND HOBBES: A CALVIN AND HOBBES TREASURY by Bill Watterson. Copyright © 1992 by Bill Watterson. Published by Andrews and McMeel, a Universal Press Syndicate Company. Used by permission.

Spot art from TYRANNOSAURUS WAS A BEAST by Jack Prelutsky, illustrated by Arnold Lobel. Illustration copyright © 1988 by Arnold Lobel. By permission of Greenwillow Books, a division of William Morrow & Company, Inc.

Cover from CHOCOLATE COVERED ANTS by Stephen Manes, illustrated by Bruce Emmett. Illustration copyright © 1990 by Scholastic Inc. Published by Scholastic Inc.

Cover from THE CYBIL WAR by Betsy Byars, illustrated by Tom Newsom. Illustration copyright © 1981 by Viking Penguin. Published by Viking Penguin, a division of Penguin Books USA Inc.

Cover from JAMES AND THE GIANT PEACH by Roald Dahl, illustrated by Chris Van Allsburg. Illustration copyright © 1988 by Viking Penguin. Published by Viking Penguin, a division of Penguin Books USA Inc.

Cover from THE STINKY CHEESE MAN by Jon Scieszka and Lane Smith, illustrated by Lane Smith. Illustration copyright © 1992 by Lane Smith. Published by Viking Penguin, a division of Penguin Books USA Inc.

Photography and Illustration Credits

Photos: © John Lei for Scholastic Inc., all Tool Box items unless otherwise noted. p. 2 cl: © Thaddeus Govan for Scholastic Inc.; bl: © John Lei for Scholastic Inc. pp. 2-3 background: © Thaddeus Govan for Scholastic Inc. p. 3 bc, c: © Thaddeus Govan for Scholastic Inc.; tc: Ana Esperanza Nance for Scholastic Inc. pp. 4-6: © Ana Esperanza Nance for Scholastic Inc. p. 28 tc: © Ana Esperanza Nance for Scholastic Inc.; all others: © Thaddeus Govan for Scholastic Inc. p. 29 br: © Steve Leonard for Scholastic Inc. p. 30 br: © Steve Leonard for Scholastic Inc. p. 31: © Thaddeus Govan for Scholastic Inc. p. 42 bl: © John Lei for Scholastic Inc. p. 43 br: © Michael Ahearn for Scholastic Inc.; © John Lei for Scholastic Inc. p. 82 tr: © Ken Karp for Scholastic Inc.; br: © John Lei for Scholastic Inc. p. 83: © John Lei for Scholastic Inc. p. 84 bc: © Stanley Bach for Scholastic Inc. p. 85 tr, cr: © John Lei for Scholastic Inc.; bl: © Stanley Bach for Scholastic Inc.; br: © Michael Ahearn for Scholastic Inc. pp. 114-115 Comic strip from the INDISPENSABLE CALVIN AND HOBBES: A CALVIN AND HOBBES TREASURY © Bill Watterson/© John Lei for Scholastic Inc. p. 116 br: © Jane Burton/Bruce Coleman, Inc. p. 117 tr: © Stanley Bach for Scholastic Inc. p. 118 br: © Jane Burton/Bruce Coleman, Inc.; bl: © John Lei for Scholastic Inc. p. 119 bl, cr: © John Lei for Scholastic Inc.; br: © Michael Ahearn for Scholastic Inc. p. 122 bc: © The Bettmann Archive. p. 124 tl: © Peter Simon; bl: © courtesy of Hikima Creations. p. 125 tr: © courtesy of Scholastic Trade Department; br: © David Godlis; cr: © courtesy of Anderson Press Ltd. London. p. 127 br: © Michael Keller/The Stock Market.

Illustrations: pp. 8-9: Michael Bartalos; pp. 10-25: Liz Callen; pp. 44-45: Julie Winston; pp. 46-48, 55, 60, 64: Rick Brown; pp. 86-87: Gary Baseman.